W9-AWR-896

STRUCTURES

SKYSCRAPERS

Andrew Dunn

Thomson Learning
New York

Titles in this series

Bridges
Dams
Skyscrapers
Tunnels

Words that appear in the glossary are printed in **bold** type the first time they appear in the text.

First published in the
United States in 1993 by
Thomson Learning
115 Fifth Avenue
New York, NY 10003

First published in 1992 by
Wayland (Publishers) Limited,
61 Western Road, Hove,
East Sussex, BN3 IJD, England

Cataloging in Publication Data applied for

ISBN 1-56847-027-4
Printed in the United States of America

Contents

1 Why we build
skyscrapers   4

2 How skyscrapers are
built   9

3 What's so good about
skyscrapers?   19

4 The down side of
building up   21

5 Skyscrapers of
tomorrow   26

Glossary   30

Books to read   31

Index   32

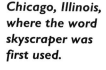

1 Why we build skyscrapers

The word skyscraper was first used in Chicago in about 1885, though nobody knows who invented it. The new buildings there were nothing like the towering, gleaming skyscrapers of today–they were only about ten floors high–but they were much taller than almost anything that had been built before.

People began building skyscrapers for several reasons. First because new **technology**, such as the discovery of how to make steel, had made it possible. And until the invention of safe, reliable passenger elevators it had not made sense to build more than four or five floors high—nobody likes climbing too many stairs!

More important, cities were getting crowded. Land for offices was becoming very expensive. The only way to make more space was to go upward. And before all our modern electronic **communication** systems were developed, office workers needed to be close to each other.

Now, more than a century later, **architects** and **civil engineers** are dreaming of ever-higher towers to pierce the sky.

Chicago, Illinois, where the word skyscraper was first used.

The Canada National Tower in Toronto rises more than 1,800 feet into the sky. It is a broadcasting tower rather than a skyscraper. You can see 75 miles from its revolving restaurant.

But now that we have computers and all kinds of communication links, workers do not all have to be in the same building. Many "office" workers already work from their homes. Furthermore, one massive sixty-floor skyscraper costs more than two buildings half the size.

However, we continue to build skyscrapers even where they are not needed. Engineers may be attracted to the adventure and challenge of building them. Tall buildings are after all unique. They really do "stand out." The very word skyscraper has an exciting, emotional ring to it.

A skyscraper can be like a small city, with shops, banks, hotels, swimming pools, movie theaters, as well as offices—all in one building. It may even have a helicopter pad on its roof.

Skyscrapers have been built for living in. Huge **apartment** buildings are just like houses stacked on top of each other—"streets in the sky." Town planners once thought apartment buildings would cure overcrowding in cities. But people do not like living far above ground, so most modern skyscrapers are built only for working in.

SKYSCRAPER ARCHITECTURE

There are many different styles of skyscrapers. Before World War II, most were faced with stone. At first, architects copied **classical** European buildings with pillars and arches. Skyscrapers were usually stepped, rising like a giant's staircase from a big base to a small point at the top. New York's Empire State Building, the tallest structure on earth in 1931, was built in this way.

Then some architects began using popular fashions in the design of skyscrapers. Art Deco, with sweeping simple lines, decorated skyscrapers like the famous 1930 Chrysler Building in New York.

WHAT ARE SKYSCRAPERS FOR?

Most skyscrapers are used as office buildings. Some are used by a single large **corporation**, while others are occupied by many smaller firms. Some have high revolving restaurants, which turn slowly as diners eat their meals and watch the changing view of the city far below. Many skyscrapers have television and **telecommunication** masts on top, taking advantage of the height to transmit over a large area.

Australia's unusual Sydney Tower is supported by strong steel cables.

New York's Chrysler Building, built in 1930, combined modern art with architecture to create an adventurous new style of building. The building is named after the car manufacturer Walter Chrysler.

In the 1950s and 1960s, simple box-like crystal skyscrapers with walls of glass swept the world. But more recently, adventurous designs, more pleasing to the eye, have appeared again. Art Deco decoration has appeared again in the Canary Wharf Tower in London's Docklands.

Built in 1990, the vast Canary Wharf Building in London's Docklands area echoes the artistic style of the Chrysler Building of sixty years earlier.

All through this book you can see pictures of different kinds of skyscrapers, built in many ways. Try designing your own skyscraper based on the style you like most. Make sketches of what it would look like from different angles.

Skyscrapers have been built with parks at street level and other features to make them nicer places for people to work in and look at. Unusual skyscrapers have appeared too; in Seattle, the Space Needle is thin, round, and 600 feet high, while the 53rd At Third building in New York, because of its elliptical shape, is sometimes called the lipstick building. The Lloyds Insurance Building in London is inside-out, with huge air ducts, elevators and stairs wrapped around the outside like drainpipes.

2 How skyscrapers are built

TECHNOLOGY THAT MADE IT POSSIBLE

People have constructed big buildings for centuries—temples, cathedrals, palaces, castles—but until little more than a century ago, they could not build very tall buildings. Early tall buildings such as castle towers had to have very thick walls at the bottom to support the weight above. A very high building would have needed such thick walls at the base that there would have been no space for rooms.

The big advance came with the discovery of steel, in the 1860s. Steel is made by adding carbon to iron, making a stronger, lighter metal.

This steel-framed building, the Auditorium, was built in 1888 in Chicago.

A skyscraper under construction in Los Angeles, California. The steel frame is already in place.

Steel was first used in building construction in a 10-floor office building in Chicago in 1885. The building was made of **cast-iron** upright columns held together by steel beams going across. The outer skin of stone was hung from this **skeleton.**

Another important technological breakthrough was the invention of a safe elevator. In 1854 Elisha Otis invented a safety clamp attached to the side of the car, which slid up and down a guide-rail in the shaft. If the support ropes went slack for any reason, the clamp gripped the rail tightly, stopping the elevator.

The first electric elevator was installed in a New York store in 1889, and push-buttons appeared five years later. When the Empire State Building opened in 1931, its express elevators rose at 1,200 ft per minute. Now elevators are capable of over 1,800 ft per minute, which is about as fast as the human body can comfortably stand.

MAKE A SKYSCRAPER FRAME
WHAT YOU NEED:
Drinking straws, short pipe cleaners.

WHAT YOU DO:
Use the pipe cleaners to join the straws together to make a framework. See how high you can go. See if a bigger base helps. Think of ways to make it stronger, still using the straws.

STARTING AT THE BOTTOM

Any structure, whether cottage or skyscraper, needs **foundations** to keep it from sinking under its own weight. Skyscrapers weigh hundreds of thousands of tons, so they need very firm foundations. New York's cramped Manhattan is lucky—it is made of solid rock, which makes an excellent foundation for the city's famous towering buildings. But most cities lie on softer ground, which explains why New York's tallest building is 1,375 ft high, while in London, built on clay, the highest reaches only 800 ft.

Skyscraper foundations can be made in several ways. If the skyscraper has a small base on soft ground, one way to support it is to spread its weight over a bigger area. This can be done by making a **raft foundation** of thousands of tons of **concrete**, much wider than the heavy building's base, underneath it. It spreads the weight and keeps the skyscraper from sinking.

Another approach is to anchor the building by pushing rods (called piles) of steel and concrete deep into the

This bell tower, built in Italy in 1350, shows what happens without firm foundations. It is now famous as "The Leaning Tower of Pisa."

ground. Like big nails hammered into wood, they have a very firm grip, especially if they can reach down to solid rock. The skyscraper is built on a concrete platform laid on top of the piles.

HOW A RAFT FOUNDATION WORKS

WHAT YOU NEED:
A thick stick, a plastic lid or round piece of strong cardboard about 4 in across, some wet sand or soil.

WHAT YOU DO:
Imagine the stick is a tall, thin skyscraper. Try to push it into the sand or soil.

Now put the plastic lid on the sand, and put the end of the stick on the middle of it. Then try to push the stick and its "foundation" into the sand.

Without the foundation, all the force of your push goes into a very small area — the size of the end of the stick. The plastic disk acts like a raft foundation, "floating" on the surface. It spreads the force of your push over a much larger area. So you have to push much harder to make it sink. Engineers can calculate the weight of a building and figure out how large the foundations must be.

Trappers in the Arctic use the same idea to keep their feet from sinking into the snow. They wear snowshoes, which look like tennis racquets tied under their feet. These spread the weight of the body, so that the feet float on the snow's surface instead of sinking.

A stick can be pushed into the sand easily because its force is concentrated.

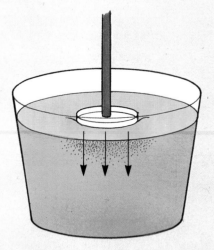

The force of the stick is spread out by the lid, so it cannot be pushed down easily.

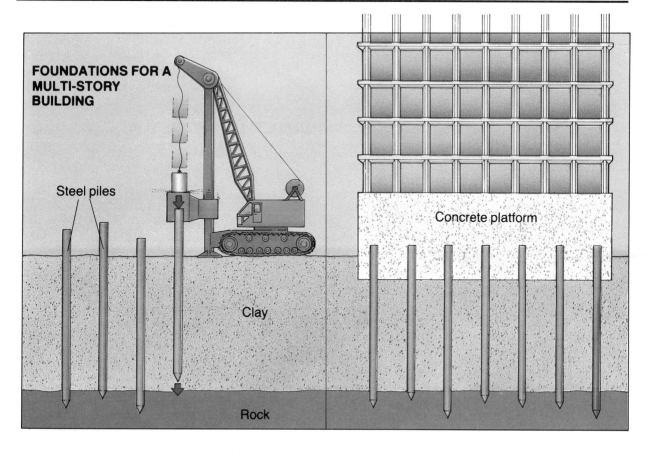

FOUNDATIONS FOR A
MULTI-STORY
BUILDING

Steel piles

Concrete platform

Clay

Rock

*A common
method of
building the
foundation for a
skyscraper, using
metal rods to
anchor it to the
ground.*

SKYSCRAPER STRUCTURES

Many skyscrapers are built with a steel framework. Light and strong, it supports the concrete floors and the walls. Others have a concrete framework, strengthened with steel rods inside the concrete beams. Some are built with a central core, a huge round column from which the floors and walls are hung. Yet another way to build is to erect several tall steel columns and lift the floors into place from the ground, one by one. The materials used must be very strong.

Steel beams and girders are made in many different shapes and can be bolted or welded together to make the framework. Diagonal girders can be used to brace the structure and make it even stronger.

Concrete is very widely used. It is made of sand and stones mixed with cement and water to glue them together. A concrete beam or column is very strong when pressed from the ends, but quite weak when bent. So concrete is usually reinforced with steel bars. The bars are put into a mold first, and then wet concrete is poured over them.

Other materials are used to make skyscraper walls. Glass walls are now

A modern pyramid—the TransAmerica building in San Francisco, California. It has sixty-one floors and is 853 feet high. Skyscrapers in San Francisco have to be able to withstand earthquakes, which occur often in the area.

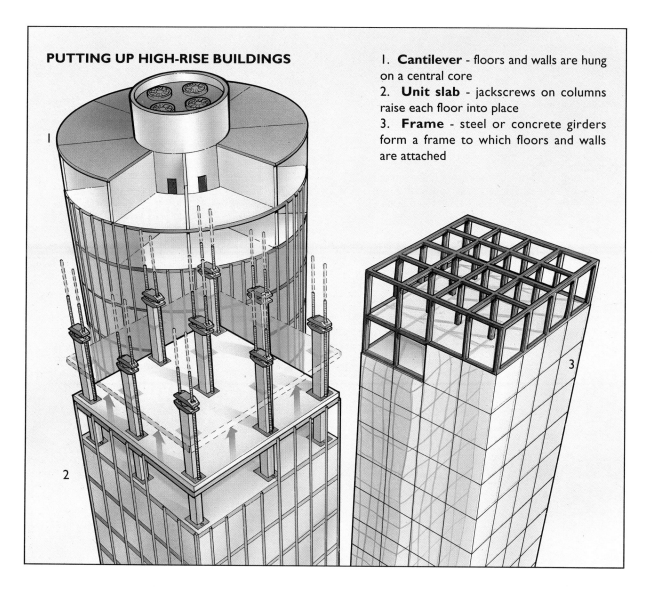

PUTTING UP HIGH-RISE BUILDINGS

1. **Cantilever** - floors and walls are hung on a central core
2. **Unit slab** - jackscrews on columns raise each floor into place
3. **Frame** - steel or concrete girders form a frame to which floors and walls are attached

quite common. Special glass is used that reflects sunlight away, which gives some buildings their mirrored look. Stainless steel is also used on skyscraper walls for a dramatic effect. Architects are always looking for new materials to use in interesting and unusual ways, to make their skyscrapers look different.

SOME SPECIAL SKYSCRAPERS

The most famous skyscraper is still the Empire State Building in New York. For 40 years, it was the world's tallest **inhabitable** building, at 1,250 ft high and with 102 floors. It consists of a simple but strong steel skeleton, with precast concrete floors and walls of masonry

BUILDING WITH NEWSPAPER

WHAT YOU NEED:

A newspaper, Scotch tape, a brick or heavy weight.

WHAT YOU DO:

You can make quite a strong tower out of thin paper. Roll a sheet into a tube, and tape it to hold it in shape. Put it upright on the floor, and try to squash it by pressing down from the top. It is surprisingly strong as a column (though it would be useless as a beam). See if it will support the brick.

Now make several more tubes of newspaper. Tape them together in a big bundle. Test the strength of your tower now.

You could try a competition with your friends, to see who can build the tallest newspaper tower in ten minutes.

and brickwork. The simple design meant that it could be built extremely quickly. The 3,500 workers added six new floors every week, and it took only 17 months from the design stage to the finished skyscraper.

In the 1980s, another massive office building used a clever design to overcome an unusual problem. It was built over Charing Cross Station, one of the busiest stations in London. The station had to carry on as usual

The Empire State Building in New York—still the world's most famous skyscraper.

The New City Hall in Tokyo, Japan, is designed like a modern version of a great medieval cathedral with two towers flanking the building's front. The building has upset some people in Japan who say it does not fit in with traditional buildings and is far too European-looking.

while it was built. Huge piles (each using 70 truckloads of concrete) were built under the platforms, in two lines 100 ft apart. On these foundations were placed columns, which rose through the platforms and the station roof to the top of the new building. Nine great arches now span the gap between the columns. The building itself hangs from these arches. Most passengers at Charing Cross are completely unaware of the office workers above their heads.

The highest self-supporting structure in the world is the Canada National Tower in Toronto. Built of reinforced concrete on three legs, it towers 1,815 ft high and weighs 143,000 tons. It has a revolving restaurant 1,140 ft above ground (from which diners can see 70 mi.). The world's highest skyscraper is the Sears Tower in Chicago, headquarters of the world's biggest retail company. It has 110 floors, reaching 1,454 ft up. Broadcasting masts take its height to 1,708 ft. It was built in 1973 by welding steel to make vertical tubes, which help to keep it from swaying from side to side. It holds 16,700 people, and has 103 elevators and 16,000 windows. The outside is covered in black aluminum and bronze-tinted glass.

The Hong Kong and Shanghai Bank in Hong Kong is similarly

Lloyds headquarters in the City of London. See how the stairs, elevators, pipes, even the building's frame, are all on the outside.

spectacular. Unlike the framework of most skyscrapers, the main frame supporting this 47-floor building can be seen from the outside. There are eight columns, each made of four tubes, and the floors are hung from five huge beams. Other buildings, like the Lloyd's Insurance Building in London, also have the frame, air conditioning ducts, and elevators all on the outside, leaving room inside for a huge open lobby space.

3 What's so good about skyscrapers?

Skyscrapers can be spectacularly beautiful. They take up much less land than low-level buildings with the same amount of room, which matters in a crowded city. This also means that developers who own very expensive land can make more money from their **investment**.

Skyscrapers allow big companies to have all their office staff in one building. Even today—with modern communications such as personal computers that talk to each other, electronic mail, **facsimile** machines, and even video-telephones—people still prefer to meet face-to-face sometimes. Using fast modern elevators, people can move from office to office within a skyscraper more easily than around several low-level buildings. It is easier, too for a person in a wheelchair to work

Sydney, Australia, has skyscrapers of many different types, shapes, and sizes.

Evening sunlight glinting off the spectacular skyscrapers of Denver, Colorado, with the Rocky Mountains behind them. Different materials are used to give buildings their own look and feel.

Try to make a list of the different groups of people who benefit from living or working in skyscrapers. Most of them will be people who have trouble getting around for some reason or people who need to be able to see each other easily and quickly.

in a skyscraper, where there are no stairs to climb or streets to cross.

Nowadays when they design buildings, architects are much more aware of the needs of people who are living with disability. Architects can build a ramp at the entrance to a building, and they can design many features inside to help people who find it hard to get around.

Skyscrapers do less damage to the **environment** we live in. One big building full of people produces less **pollution** than many small buildings containing the same number of people. All the main services—air-conditioning, heating, water—can be run from one place.

In modern skyscrapers, technology that saves energy is used, so that less electricity and less fuel are needed. Special window glasses have been developed, which can change color if the sun is too bright and absorb or reflect heat (keeping the inside at a comfortable temperature).

4 The down side of building up

Like any big structures, sky-scrapers have their drawbacks. They tower over the local area. If care is not taken over their appearance, they can look like big ugly boxes. Skyscrapers are very expensive. Most, however, are built to last a long time, which is just as well since they are difficult to demolish if they become unsafe.

The huge numbers of workers entering and leaving a skyscraper every day can make nearby side-walks very crowded. Workers need extra trains and buses to reach the building from their homes. If they drive, the streets will be thronged with traffic—and where will they park their cars? All these and other problems must be considered before a skyscraper is built. Building skyscrapers makes sense only if it saves land for other good purposes such as housing or public parks, or if it helps to keep the city from sprawling into the countryside.

Skyscrapers can make someone on the sidewalk feel very small indeed. Sunlight hardly reaches the streets.

At first, replacing city slums with modern-looking buildings seemed like a good idea. People could live close to their work, enjoying cheap heat and electricity. But in reality it turned out that people felt cut off and lonely. Elevators broke down. The grocery store could be a long walk. Children had nowhere to play where their parents could keep an eye on them. So now, new housing is more likely to be in the form of houses or low-rise apartment complexes.

SAFETY IN SKYSCRAPERS

Very tall buildings have problems that do not affect ordinary buildings as much. Safe design and construction are important. Disasters do happen, usually because of a fault in construction or because the designer got some calculations wrong.

All failures of design or construction are carefully analyzed afterward to see what happened, so that the same mistakes are not repeated. In the 1960s a gas explosion in an apartment building in London blew out a wall in one apartment. It brought other apartments crashing down. As a result, the style of construction used there was never used again.

Fire can be very dangerous in a tall building, for obvious reasons. Escape by stairs may take a long time even if they are

Apartments like these in Barcelona, Spain, may be noisy, with neighbors above and below as well as next door.

During the 1960s, it was fashionable to build high-rise apartment buildings. As technology advanced it became cheaper to build very high buildings. Fewer workers were needed to build big apartment buildings than were needed to build houses for the same number of people. And cheaper buildings meant lower rents, which families could afford.

There are some accidents that a designer cannot foresee, but from which lessons can still be learned. One foggy afternoon in 1945, a B25 bomber crashed into the side of the Empire State Building. The crew and twelve office workers inside were killed, but the building did not suffer major damage. Now all tall buildings carry warning lights. The enormous towers of the World Trade Center in New York were built to withstand the impact of a Boeing 707, the largest airliner of the time.

not blocked by fire, and the windows are much too high to jump from. So elaborate fire detection equipment and sprinklers are built into all big modern buildings.

EARTHQUAKE AND WIND

In many parts of the world earthquakes are quite common. Skyscraper cities prone to earthquakes include Oakland, San Francisco, and Los Angeles in California, and the big cities of Japan. So far though, no modern skyscraper has collapsed in an earthquake, but older, smaller buildings have fallen around them.

A skyscraper in an earthquake area must be able to withstand up-and-down vibrations, and side-to-side vibrations that are more serious. During earthquakes, ground that seemed solid can turn to something like jelly or even liquid, so solid foundations are extremely important.

Several anti-earthquake features have been designed into tall buildings in recent years. One of the most successful has been the use of big rubber springs under the skyscraper. They

Skyscrapers have to be able to withstand the shock of an earthquake that would cause other buildings to collapse.

absorb the vibrations of earthquakes much as a car's shock absorbers smooth out bumps in the road.

All skyscrapers must withstand wind. A thousand feet or more above ground, wind has great power. So a tall, slender skyscraper has to be flexible and bend in the wind, or it would be pushed over. The top of a tall skyscraper may sway more than three feet on a windy day. People working there may not notice that, but they can often hear the building creak!

One way of coping with the wind is to make the building itself react. Blocks of concrete weighing hundreds of tons are placed on rollers

Think what it would be like to work or live at the top of a skyscraper. Think about the disadvantages. They might have to do with safety, machinery in the skyscraper breaking down, or the number of people living in a small space.

Write a story about what it's like to live in a sky-scraper, using the things you have thought about from this box and the one on page 20.

in a big room at the top of the build-ing. As the wind pushes the build-ing in one direction, the natural reaction of the heavy weight is to roll the other way. This helps to keep the building relatively still, "damping" the wind's force.

5 Skyscrapers of tomorrow

HOW HIGH CAN WE GO?

This is almost a silly question. If someone wanted to build a skyscraper as high as Mount Everest, it could be done—as long as the base was wide enough, and there was enough money! A tall, fat building is easy. A tall, thin building is much more difficult. Most skyscrapers are slender, because they are built on small sites.

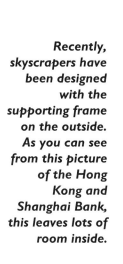

Recently, skyscrapers have been designed with the supporting frame on the outside. As you can see from this picture of the Hong Kong and Shanghai Bank, this leaves lots of room inside.

Skyscrapers already tower higher than seems possible, but they could go up even farther. This is the World Financial Center in New York.

THE LIMITS OF TECHNOLOGY

As buildings grow taller they become heavier. Engineers have to be very precise, even with the latest advanced materials and technology. A steel frame is compressed under the weight of the floors above, by about $\frac{1}{16}$ in per floor. Concrete also "creeps" slowly, shrinking by about the same amount over five years. A skyscraper also grows in the heat of the day, and shrinks during the cooler night. Engineers have to allow for this kind of thing in their calculations.

The problems of building skyscrapers increase with height. More weight means bigger, stronger foundations and a frame made of stronger, lighter materials. But architects and civil engineers like adventurous new challenges. They are always eager to try new ideas for exciting skyscrapers, higher than would have seemed possible before.

There probably are limits, though. A building is no use if people have to spend all day in an elevator—an unpopular place. If you have been in one, you may have noticed that people don't speak much or look at one another. Some have suggested making a bigger, more comfortable elevator, like a small lounge. But there is still a limit to how fast elevators can travel, not because of the machinery, but because of people's physical limitations.

Here, in an office building in the UK, tinted mirrored glass has been used to great effect.

The fastest speed at which people will comfortably bear being lifted straight upwards is about 33 ft per second, about 22 mph. Reaching the top of a 100-floor skyscraper would take about a minute, even at that speed. And the speed downward has to be even slower, because the increasing air pressure makes people's ears pop. One idea is to build a cableless elevator, which would travel up tracks in the shaft, like a railroad on its side. It would probably be safer than the traditional elevator in a very tall building.

The highest office building in the world, the Sears Tower in Chicago, is 100 floors high. Going higher will mean inventing new technology, but engineers are convinced they can do it. Some think the next very tall skyscraper will be about 150 floors high — say 2,000-2,300 feet. Others think there is no limit, and talk of skyscrapers like complete cities, 5,000 or even 10,000 feet high. The tops would be above the clouds, truly scraping the sky.

Chicago, Illinois, is home to the world's tallest skyscraper—the 1,454-foot Sears Tower. The television masts on top take it to over 1,700 feet.

Glossary

Apartment A set of rooms, usually on one floor, for living in. In some places, apartments are called flats.

Architects People who design buildings of all kinds and see that the plans are carried out by the builders.

Cast iron Iron metal mixed with carbon, which is poured when molten into a mold of whatever shape is needed.

Civil engineer Someone who designs buildings and structures that are used by the public, or who makes sure that they continue to be safe for people to use.

Classical In the style of ancient Greece or Rome. Painting, architecture, writing, acting, and many other things can be classical in style.

Communication The giving or exchanging of information by any means, such as speaking directly to someone else, by sending a letter, or using the telephone or fax machine.

Concrete A very strong building material made of sand and small stones, mixed with a glue of cement and water. Wet concrete is poured into molds, usually made on the building site, to make beams and columns; or it is poured into holes to make foundation piles. Concrete sets hard in about a day.

Corporation A large business firm, often working in several countries.

Environment Everything around us, including the air we breathe, the land we live on, and the water we drink.

Facsimile (Pronounced "fac-*sim*-ill-ee"). An exact copy. People use facsimile machines (known as fax machines) to send and receive exact copies of paper documents (called faxes) to and from other fax machines anywhere in the world.

Foundation The solid base on which a building stands.

Inhabitable Suitable for people to live in.

Investment Money that has been put to work to produce more money, whether in a savings account at a bank or in a profitable project such as building a new factory.

Pollution The waste gases, liquids and solids that poison our surroundings (the environment) and harm or even kill plants and animals.

Raft foundation A flat platform which "floats" on the surface, distributing the weight of the building above it.

Skeleton A frame inside a structure (like the bones inside your body).

Technology Science as it is applied in practical work.

Telecommunication The sending of messages over a great distance, mostly by telephone or radio. Telecommunication often involves bouncing radio signals off satellites in space.

BOOKS TO READ

Buildings, Bridges and Tunnels, by Angela Royston. Tell Me About (New York: Warwick, 1991).

Cities: Citizens & Civilization, by Fiona Macdonald (New York: Franklin Watts, 1992).

Grand Constructions, by Gian Paolo Ceserani (New York: Putnam, 1983).

Structures and Materials, by Barbara Taylor (New York: Franklin Watts, 1991).

Index

Numbers printed in **bold** refer to pictures
as well as text.

architectural styles 6-8
Auditorium, Chicago **9**

Barcelona, Spain **22**

Canada National Tower, Canada **5**, 18
Canary Wharf, Britain **8**
Charing Cross Station, Britain 16, 18
Chicago, Illinois **4, 9,** 18, **29**
Chrysler Building, New York **3, 7,** 8
communications 5, 6, 19
concrete 11, 13
construction methods 13, **15**-18

dangers to skyscrapers
    earthquake 24-25
    wind 25
Denver, Colorado **20**

elevators 4, 10, 18, 19, 28-29

PICTURE ACKNOWLEDGMENTS
The artwork on pages 13 and 15 was provided
by Nick Hawken, and the artwork on page 12
was provided by Steve Wheele.

The publishers gratefully acknowledge permis-
sion from the following to reproduce their
pictures in this book: Eye Ubiquitous 24, 25;
Mountain Camera (John Cleare) 6, 14, 18, 19,
26, 28; Peter Newark 9; Tony Stone
Worldwide 4, 20, 29; Zefa 5, 7, 10, 11, 16, 17,
21, 22, 23.

Empire State Building, New York 15-**16, 23**
    airplane crashing into 23
environmental impact of skyscrapers 20

53rd At Third, New York 8
foundations 11, **12, 13**

Hong Kong and Shanghai Bank,
    Hong Kong 18, 26

Lloyds Insurance Building, Britain 8, **18**
London, England **18,** 22
Los Angeles, California **10**, 24

New York, New York **4, 6, 8**
    Manhattan 11

Pisa, leaning tower, Italy **11**

safety features 22-25

San Francisco earthquake 24
Sears Tower, Chicago 18, **29**
Space Needle, Seattle 8
steel 9-10, 13
    rods to strengthen concrete 11-12
Sydney, Australia **19**
    Sydney Tower, **6**

Tokyo New City Hall, Japan **17**
TransAmerica Building, San Francisco **14**

World Financial Center, New York, **27**